HEAT

Series 3 Number 9

Sarah Mosca
Echo XI 2022
xerograph
51 × 41 cm (framed)
courtesy of the artist and
Sarah Cottier Gallery, Sydney

Sarah Mosca's suite of works
titled *Echo I – XII* includes twelve
xerograph reproductions, each fixed
on the gesture of women's hands
captured in a range of actions to
emphasise the body language of
labour. Her xerographs (Greek for
'dry writing') are produced without
the use of liquid chemicals, bringing
a certain texture to the historical
records she recontextualises. She
says of the works: 'Hand gestures
are a form of non-verbal, nuanced
language. We notice people's hands
and read them based on an applied
set of codes... Selected from a library
of open-source photographs, each
of my re-compositions focus only
on hands in action (or inaction);
gestures of balancing, mending,
desire, idleness...these actions are
removed from their context. Each
gesture varies in meaning, yet
focused on substitute readings.'

ALENA LODKINA
TWO STORIES

Alena Lodkina is a Russian-born Australian filmmaker. She directed and co-wrote her first feature film *Strange Colours* (2017), which debuted at Venice Film Festival. *Petrol* (2022), her second feature film as writer and director, premiered at Locarno Film Festival and later screened at the 52nd edition of New Directors/New Films presented by the Museum of Modern Art and Film at Lincoln Centre in New York. She has made fiction and documentary short films, and has written about film. These two stories, first drafted in 2015, explore themes that were later developed in *Petrol*.

A Beautiful Girl, A Beautiful Dress

I spent a few years working in cafés after graduating from art school. I didn't see what else I could do. The work kept me moving, I was fed, had nice coffees and beers and wines, and most of all I enjoyed the many faces constantly passing in front of my eyes. The conversations were mostly silly and forgettable, which I liked. All I had to do was to keep opening my mouth, to smile and to keep my feet moving. Everything was moving. Plates were flying, cups wobbling on saucers, knives splicing, forks lifting with vigour, spoons diving from heights. So for a while, I could afford to live in Melbourne and was distracted from the more violent and gloomy thoughts that started to creep around my heart.

One of these cafés was called Zaika's, it was a local favourite. It was a bakery owned by an old Ukrainian woman. I liked her because whenever she spoke about something she would open her eyes wide, point her index finger upwards and come really close to your face, and in that moment, as she remembered excitedly a little salacious anecdote from her past, she seemed like a young woman. She loved her customers and couldn't say no to anyone, she loved to please. The bread and the cakes baked there were very good. At midday she would take an olive loaf out of the oven, rip it open and dip bits in mayonnaise, telling stories as she chewed. She had a lot of life in her and had a sharp tongue, and occasionally her comments would reveal a ruthless streak common in business people.

What I really liked was looking at some little old lady or a crooked old gentleman squeezed in at a small table, as they cut open their generous slice of lemon tart, smothered a sweet spoonful in cream, and put it in their agape mouth, triggering waves of delight across their face.

We, the waitresses, loved talking about sex, whenever there was a lull. *So last night he asked me to bite his*, she'd lower her voice, *dick, and I just couldn't bring myself to do it. I really respect him for being able to ask me that sort of thing, but it felt cruel.* We'd tell her to do it. Or we'd discuss straightness and queerness. Some of the girls loved men, others didn't. The owner didn't like the waitresses to have boyfriends. She thought that young men were useless lovers. What she really didn't like was when one of us would come into work sour, or better yet, in tears, because of some guy – that happened all the time. *He just fucked off and left me to deal with the apartment totally on my own, and I hear he's already seeing someone else, it's so fucked up*, one of us would explain. We'd hug her and let her take longer breaks and have glasses of wine throughout the shift. One waitress, who was older than all of us, had no illusions about men. *You'd be best off if you expect nothing*, she'd say with a heavy air. I loved listening to her sharp black-and-white thoughts. Now, I can hardly remember the feeling, but back then my own heart was often seized by some sadness connected with a man, or a lack of a man.

It was on a busy lunchtime that I first noticed her, standing in a line and waiting for a sandwich. I never found out what her name actually was but I think it was Natasha, well, she struck me as Natasha. Maybe it's not very interesting but the reason I noticed her that day was because she was wearing this dress, very simple, very elegant. Elephant grey, it was a soft expensive material – a blend of linen and silk – which for me was a mark of exceptional taste. It was the sort of colour that you could rest your eyes on, let your worries and agitations glide over. Maybe it wasn't only the colour and the fabric, but the way it wrapped her body, which was beautiful. The dress fell loosely off her shoulders, and picked her up at her waist, as though she was held by another's effortless hand.

I noticed the dress first, but then I started looking at this Natasha. It is not often that I can say this about someone, but I felt sure that everyone would agree that she was beautiful. Okay, we know that beauty is in the eye of the beholder, but this woman was unarguably beautiful, I don't know how else to put it. In her wonderful garment, lean like a gazelle, breasts shaped like perfect tear drops, small ankles, skin like an untouched forest. Not her hips, or shoulders, or ears, or her nose – nothing in her was grotesque. And yet she was not boring. She leaned against the wall, looking out into space, and I noticed that her big full lips were moving a little, murmuring something absentmindedly. It felt to me that she couldn't be conceited or guarded, and that somehow her physicality expressed the inner logic of her being. She got her chicken sandwich, made some small joke and walked out of the café. *She was really beautiful*, I said to the other girls, *yeah she really was*, they confirmed.

Natasha kept coming in to get a sandwich a few times a week. I noticed that she had some flaws – for example her feet were quite large and she had a heavy walk, like a penguin – but it made me like her even more, just enough of a flaw to make her seem real. At first I was really eager to serve her, hoping that by having contact with her, I too would grow to be more beautiful, as though she were a rejuvenating spa. But after a while I grew tired. I wasn't becoming more beautiful but was simply becoming more aware of my own self, and I let the other girls serve her. I had awkwardly shaped hips, little hands with short sausage

11

fingers, mousy hair, average face, I was clumsy and my clothes were dirty and worn. I owned a few nice things but I rarely wore them because I was afraid of drawing attention to myself.

I loved the sorts of things Natasha wore, always simple, unpretentious and also unusual. She wore things that were flattering but didn't over-emphasise her exceptional body. One day it'd be a large light blue shirt tucked into old-fashioned pants that hugged her hips like a wave, or a black velvet jumpsuit, or a long silk dress that tied around her torso, a high-waisted skirt with some small loose blue top or a satin silvery long-sleeve one; she'd throw on a linen scarf, she'd have silver rings on her neat fingers. Her long thick black hair fell off her head like a cliff dropping into an ocean. My favourite thing remained her elephant-coloured dress.

Through the regularity with which she came in, I knew she worked a full-time job – some kind of an office. There were various kinds of 'nice' offices that existed in the neighbourhood, creative studios with lots of natural light, plants and ping-pong tables. People in these offices seemed to me akin to princes and princesses in castles, clean and crisp. I didn't know if Natasha liked her job, but she seemed happy when she came in to buy her lunch, and she must have had a decent wage to afford to buy lunch so often, as well as all her clothes. I liked that she ate sandwiches.

Sometimes she came in with a guy and they sat down for lunch together. He was extremely handsome and the girls immediately started flirting with him, but Natasha didn't show jealous discomfort. I wasn't enamoured with this guy, but I liked him. He too had a lean, attractive body and nice clothes, was funny and well-spoken and polite to us. Sometimes he would look at his phone for a little too long. Natasha would very lightly tap his wrist and he would smile and put his phone away.

One day I was walking around the streets. After work I often didn't want to go home, where little would happen and where there was that thick grey carpet, my loud chatty housemates and their sad and lazy dog, and my tiny room with my laughable possessions. Instead I dragged out afternoons by walking around the neighbourhood, looking at shopfronts and galleries. By then my ambitions of becoming an artist had left me, but I didn't lose an aesthetic appreciation. My own lack of talent and will didn't prevent me from being able to feel joy at others' gifts and abilities. So many pretty things were always on display. For example there was a craze about artistic ceramic objects, pastel-coloured, clunky and funny; somehow they made you feel closer to people. I wanted to pick up an object like that and hold it in my hands, but a fear would pervade me that I could break it and would have to pay for it, so I rarely did. In a gallery I'd see a smooth round white ball, or a piece of delicate see-through fabric stretched out and lit from one side, or lots of tiny photographs stuck onto a black wall in a neat order, or pieces of paper covered with writing spread out on the floor, or some kind of video flashing on a big screen, or a small screen, and sounds, hard and soft, coming from the ceiling or the walls. I'd smile and feel modest, pleasant emotions rise in my heart.

It was then that I found it – the dress. I turned into a street where I had never gone and saw a small clothing store. It was peaceful inside. The walls were dark and the shop was intimately lit, just enough to see the garments, but not enough to be horrified at the sight of oneself. The garments were few, swaying on the racks like melancholic birds. I saw it right away, Natasha's dress. Incredibly, it was in the sale section, fifty per cent off. I couldn't believe it. I flicked through the pieces: they had my size. Everything happened extremely fast. It was as though I was operating in a dream. I took the dress into the dressing room, made sure it fit me, paid for it, and practically flew home, carried by wings of must-have-been-fate.

In my room, I ripped off all my clothes and stared at my naked body in the mirror in the fading evening light. It didn't seem terrible, my body, it was shapely. I put on the dress. I liked it on me, it was flattering and felt comfortable. I lay on my bed and closed my eyes, holding myself in my arms.

For a few moments, my head was completely empty, as though there was nothing in the world and I was floating in a blurry expanse. I thought of how I too was a penguin, in ice-cold water, swimming to some distant shore. Nothing, nothing, nothing – I, a small lone penguin. And then it came – in a turgid rush, unbearable, violent, horrible, horrible. What was it? Walls collapsing like cardboard, my bed dissolving, all the books and clothes and pots and pens and shoes and shelves in my room crumbling, disintegrating; where, who was willing this, where was I? What was this pain coming over me? Despair inside? Or outside? I clutched the sheets, I was sweating, I realised that the sheets were wet, I was weeping.

I saw Natasha: gigantic and powerful, like Athena, her colossal arms spread out, her fragile smile and her enormous lips, murmuring. She was moving towards me as though descending from the sky. I fucking hated her. I wanted to grip her in my hands and shake her, a dull doll that I never wanted to play with. I knew something: I had been unhappy but I hadn't known despair, I had known bitterness but I had never known hatred.

In an instant, I was changed. This female spectre was stifling me and I couldn't breathe. I caught a fragment of my own face in the mirror – I was – beautiful? Disgustingly. A waxed green apple with no qualities. Gripping my face, I rocked backwards, falling, I forgot that I had a body at all. My eyes shut helplessly, salty hair stuck in my mouth, jaw tight like a shell of an oyster.

I fell asleep. And when I woke up, I had forgotten a part of myself forever. That really is possible, despite what they say.

Years passed. I never would have guessed that things would work out for me. I got a job, moved out on my own, met a man, etc., etc. I got all the things. Now I'm pleased with myself. After I bought the dress, I never saw Natasha again. Sometimes I still think of her – where is she now? It doesn't matter. I wear that dress to parties, and people tell me I look beautiful.

An Old Friend

1.

I was afraid. I heard myself speak. I was speaking and listening, I was doing it fine, but the whole experience was unpleasant. I did not want to sound like that (coarse, vulgar, even my throat felt as though it was full of sand); I wanted to say something different, to lead us towards at least a single pure thought, or to be led there by this woman. Instead, we were circling around, repeating ourselves.

'He was so manipulative, and it took me almost ten years to realise. It was an abusive relationship! Not physically, but emotionally – hard to pin down.'

'He was manipulative, he was abusive,' I echoed. I did not know this man, but yes, perhaps I did know.

'He was manipulative, he was abusive, he...he made me feel...he ruined me for years, he made me feel – nothing but a vast emptiness. He made a rat out of me, he...I tried to ignore it, I hate to put blame on people; but one morning I woke up as though pinned to my bed by a cold iron on my chest, and I thought, every morning I wake up like this. And I just cannot believe that I let a man change me.'

'Let's go, let's get out of here,' I stood up and banged the empty beer glass against the wooden bench. I couldn't stand it anymore. I lifted my arm like a captain and cut through a cloud of smoke that was perched above us. She lifted her big sad eyes, rose in steady motion as though lifted by a rope, and followed, her body limp and servile. As we squeezed through the groups standing by the bar, I saw men's heads lift and many beady glistening eyes fix on us, like frogs watching out for flies.

'Let's go, let's go,' I mumbled.

Once we were out of there, Daisy covered her face with her hands and started rapidly talking in a monotone stream. The sky had a dirty shade of red at the bottom where it met the brick buildings, the air wasn't fresh, yet it was still better to be outside than inside. Through Daisy's hands I was catching sharp little fragments: 'I never should've said anything, please don't tell anyone, especially the sex stuff, he was a beautiful man, you know I didn't mean any of it, you understand what love does to you.' I put my arms around her shoulders and led us down the street, and in that moment I thought her stupid and weak, but I longed to love her and I knew that if I judged her I would make my own life unbearable for myself. A cab pulled by and we got in to be taken to the beach, and Daisy continued hiding her face in her hands. I spent whole minutes inspecting what I could glimpse of my face in the driver's mirror. No matter how long I spent hoping to see my own face, I never could. We were both so absorbed in the course of our evening neither of us took note of who the driver was, but that's what we paid for, a choice to discard even the most basic human decency.

We got to the beach. 'Let's swim,' I said. Daisy didn't want to swim, it was a cold night and we didn't have our swimmers on, but I was unstoppable. Normally I hate swimming in the ocean, everything about it scares me deeply; but after a few drinks I dive in fearlessly, with abandon and hope. I took all my clothes off and plunged myself in, frolicking in the waves like an awkward fat salmon. Later on, I'd be proud of this. Daisy freed her face from her hands and sat on the shore, silently fingering the sand and doing her best not to weep. The cold water sobered me up, reminding me of my laughable situation. 'Daisy! Daisy!' I cried.

2.

I didn't see her the next day. She wasn't really a friend. We saw each other maybe once a year, whenever she had trouble with men. She could never figure it out, she was often lonely. I was lonely too, but I'd been lonely for a long time. On the weekend she called me again, which was unusual, 'What are you doing tonight?' Nothing. 'Nothing comes out of nothing, nothing adds up to a long nothing, doesn't it,' she said thoughtfully, and she also mentioned feeling stupid about the other night, talking and talking like that. I told her there was no need, I don't judge her, though I said that mainly to appease her as of course I did judge her, as all sane persons judge each other daily, meticulously and without regret. She suggested we do something civilised, like watch a movie. Okay!

That evening at my house I put on an old noir film for her, it was called *Laura*, and in it a male detective investigating a murder of a beautiful, talented young woman, spends a day and night at her lavish apartment, smelling her clothes, reading her diaries and letters, and staring at her portrait, and he rapidly falls in love with her. The detective is hard and blank, and the absent woman is soft and blank, and the love that grows out of this blank collision is very strange, but entirely enviable. The apartment in the film is full of exceptional objects that fill the frame: little decorative bottles, a mosaic cigarette case, ancient vases, an attractive clock, lamps, curtains and paintings, and many more big and little things. 'Life is not like this,' suddenly said Daisy. 'Days and hours stretch out and you wait for someone to love you, but where are you all that time? Ah men, all these men.' I looked at her. She laughed. She was delicate and giraffe-like, with a long pale neck and waves of chestnut hair. Her lips were always an unnatural dark pink, as though she had just eaten a handful of raspberries, and her eyes were big like soup bowls, bowls that scooped up memories and feelings and stewed them. She had a strange voice, it had so many shades to it that it was impossible to remember; you couldn't bring up her voice in your head. I admired her beauty and I wanted something like that. I didn't think that I was beautiful, though it is hard to make that kind of judgement about oneself. She fell asleep on the left side of my bed, and as I was falling asleep on the right side, I imagined that her legs were my legs, that her lashes were my lashes, her ears my ears. In the morning she complimented me on the tastefulness of my apartment, and my humble approach to materialism; I would think about this comment in the years to come with much pleasure.

3.

We saw each other two more times. The first time was when we went to the symphony and I fell asleep for ten minutes in the middle section of the performance, a fairly standard and boring rendering of some Schubert hits. 'Drinks! Drinks!' we were both excited about drinks at the intermission. Again, she talked of the legacy of her abusive relationship and we tried to solve it together, but we ended exactly at the point where we started, the previous time. These discussions are not about solutions, they are never solution-oriented; such discussions are in themselves poetic structures, with sinuous passageways that sometimes connect to lower and higher planes and sometimes turn back onto themselves, and in these discussions a participant must give in to the rhythms and the tones, therefore repeating certain statements over and over again (he was abusive, he was manipulative). The statements don't mean anything. The discussions are pretzels, and one must console oneself with the pretzel's soft curves.

The second time I saw her was at a party. We went there because Daisy knew that there would be several young men attending. I was in an irritable mood and hardly opened my mouth. Daisy lit up, because the truth is, she absolutely adored the company and attention of men. When there were men around, she liked looking at the men as she talked, and for a long time I didn't like going out with her if I knew there'd be men present, I wanted to be with her on my own, until I came to expect it and started to enjoy looking at her, looking at the men. She made sure to tell her stories quickly, looking the men in the eyes, and they listened and smiled. She drank, she talked, she looked the men in the eyes, she returned many of the men's smiles. 'Goodbye,' I squeezed her elbow, 'have a nice night.' 'Goodbye darling.' Daisy couldn't hide her secret pleasure at being left alone amongst the men.

4.

I thought about Daisy a lot, but not always with pleasure; I thought about her diligently, earnestly. I valued her immensely, but I didn't trust her. I wanted to love her completely, but it's hard to love someone you can't trust. Maybe she was just being careful.

The last time I heard from her was when she called me some time later: 'It's going well,' she said. 'Before, I didn't even know it was possible, it existed, such niceness. But it does! It does! I had cold feet at first, and he was so upset, that sweet man, but now... Now, things are going swimmingly. We both have our lives, you know. Very independent. That's because I can really trust him. I could even have another lover, or let him have a lover – it's that kind of relationship, we just trust each other. But we'll see. How are you?' I looked out the window of my room. The front garden was a sinister boxed space with weeds and grasses taking over the little designated area of soil. In those weeds and grasses there were snails, worms, slugs, caterpillars, bugs, I don't know. I had many days stretch out in front of me, the days would soon fill with words, exposing the contours of passing time, and I would keep trying to remember my own face. 'I'm pretty good,' I said.

MARIANNE BORUCH
THREE POEMS

Marianne Boruch is an American poet and essayist whose work has appeared in *The New Yorker*, *London Review of Books*, *Axon* and elsewhere. Her eleventh collection, *Bestiary Dark*, resulted from her observations of Australian wildlife while a 2019 Fulbright Scholar hosted by International Poetry Studies Institute at the University of Canberra. Among her honours are the Kingsley Tufts Poetry Award for *The Book of Hours*, as well as fellowships from the Guggenheim Foundation, Rockefeller's Bellagio Centre, MacDowell, Yaddo, The American Academy in Rome, and Denali and Isle Royale national parks.

Masterclass
for Henry Kramer

Two hours or so,
his jacket too small,
                    a piano nerd

he says of himself.
Is he amused
                    by his own caption?

Because the mask,
the covid mask...
                    I'm not really the secret

I look to be either.
Behind mine, you can't tell
                            my mouth might

be ready to hold forth how
others in this room too
                            only seem

to be blanks, the quiet of confetti
post-heartbreak-parade.
                            There.

I'll say it: No wisdom
at a piano like this much anymore,
                            this nerd

whose fingers under, over,
up ceiling and down
               make a point,

that can't be unmade.
Or it's me who can't quite
                  except

the arm, *the arm*
is your breath,
            he says as if

black and white keys,
a massive intake
          of dark under dark

is breath out and landing right now, right here.
That's the gist, the gift
             of a thing

in a masterclass
between bouts of immense
             not-knowing

and early March,
always a slow refreeze,
              what's old as snow, its

I-can't-do-this-anymore.
And beyond, what
            in the boy at

his Chopin for the piano nerd—
play it, play it!—
                              is a side thing, philosophy

his real love at the college
which must surely be
                              pinning a flag

no one will see to a life raft,
like a composer
                              too soon, too early

goes faint then fainter, his TB
leaving behind a sound that
                              doubles and triples

and wonders and stops.
The brilliant piano nerd tells us
                              through the boy—

boy as wind tunnel, as glass
that magnifies—*do you know this?*
                              Did you know already

Chopin still young, no time to do
one blessed thing more?
                              We eavesdroppers

will never again sleep past
the 19th century
                              without this beauty

burning up, spilling
through his hands.
                    Those *Preludes...*

mystery and dust close
as the turn of a key
                    unlocking a door.

I listened as the dead listen which may be
how Chopin—
                    You can't shake it, can you?

Practice

I held the needle so the thread could find it, my hand
swimming at me to do
my grandmother's bidding. It made me practically
cross-eyed. But she could not see
to see anything, she said. Late afternoons lost
to her needles welcoming so many colours
just in case, to stock up since
my visit was short, lasting only a childhood.

From her daybed window, I'd look out to where
I watched a solar eclipse, 'watch' not exactly,
given the *do not look* involved.
Of course, of course...
Maybe that really was enough, the whole slow yard's
full light turned sudden dark as
crickets you hear to see.

I did run thread through each eye,
knotted each end once, then twice, lined up
the needles on a green piece of felt
she'd cut. I laid them down straight, never to know
or care to know what they
might bring together, the small fate
of button to shirt, ripped
pocket-of-the-lost-key no longer,
a hem back in place.

When I sew now in the rare of an evening,
it's her needle and her
black thread, my aim like hers
all over the place. Our try
and try again— Our so many times,
that one eye between us.

Ancient World
at the American Academy, Rome

Over the library, you sleep.

Over bones that rest in books below
minus heart and all muscle, minus how they
moved the ancient world
right now. Remember? That walk through
Herculaneum, that
sandal left behind an hour ago, 86 BCE.

All these things left behind.

One thinks to sleep in a bed
is called dreaming.
One sleeps through a lifetime called
eyes shut open.

All things left behind.

Old apartment at night, glorious
flat above a library, words
one floor down float up—
prophecy city wall pickpocket saint...
You next to me again or me
next to you, windows multiplied to a vast

few stars. Some future fog
in the making.

BONNY CASSIDY
MEMORY BOOK

Bonny Cassidy is the author of three collections of poetry and co-editor of the anthology *Contemporary Australian Feminist Poetry*. Her debut collection, *Certain Fathoms*, was shortlisted for the 2012 Western Australian Premier's Poetry Award, and *Chatelaine* was shortlisted for the 2018 Prime Minister's Literary Award for Poetry and the 2018 Queensland Literary Award for Poetry. Bonny teaches Creative Writing at RMIT University and lives in the bush on Dja Dja Wurrung Country, Central Victoria. Her first book of prose, *Monument*, will be published later this year.

He goes he goes he goes he just goes

The evening nurse calls to say he's had a fall. That phrase – the traditional signpost of the sudden demise.

I was out with Mum when the call came. Mum, who had that very afternoon moved her entire life from Cronulla, to my town of Castlemaine. Dad doesn't fall ever and then the day she skips town after forty years – unbeknownst to him, who no longer knows where he is or that he is separated from her or that they sold their house – he falls.

It's been like this the last few years: the thin veil of symbols and correspondences fluttering over our lives.

When I call the ward back in the morning, I speak to a different nurse who says an X-ray showed nothing. *He's leaning on the table right now, looking at me*, she says. *Want to speak to him?* This with a bit of a giggle. *No thank you*, I say and we have a laugh. I'm pleased by the image of him leaning casually against that dining table in the common area, awaiting instruction from the switchboard behind the thick perspex window of the nurse's station.

Oftentimes he believes he is at work. They said to me a month or so ago that it'd be best if family visited in the mornings, since the afternoon prompts him to begin packing up his bag in preparation to join his colleagues and head home.

I text C with the news about the fall and the negative X-ray and the chipper report. *So one fall and he's fixed?* C shoots back. The available emojis don't really offer the sort of mirth I want to express.

The best part of it all has been this absurd and mean humour amongst we the living. I didn't know a little streak of meanness could run through loving care like that.

While I'm writing this I find my right hand turning the ring

35

finger on my left, as though I'm trying to unscrew it. The pale indentation of a band is still just visible after four months. I end up gently pinching the base of the finger, a sort of caress. I catch myself doing this about once a week, though I wonder how often I do it unconsciously.

Shapes

Because of the cover redesign I don't even recognise *Tracks* amongst the magazines in the newsagent. I was looking for those tall capitals and the standard portrait format; now it's all sans serif, lower case and with the square format of a culture mag; no more G-string butts on every second page.

In primary school, I cut out one of those babes and glued it to a letter that my friend and I were sending to some stranger. It was pre-internet, I think the guy was my friend's distant cousin. *Here's a recent photo of me from a beach shoot*, we wrote. Our modelling career was taking off and we looked forward to his reply. We could hardly believe that not only was his reply promptly sent, but that he'd offered himself up to us with a rapturous, drooling grin. It was as though a pair of ten-year-olds had just found a large ornate key that they didn't really want.

I present Dad with the magazine thinking it's going to make his day. I point out the new look. *Woah,* he says but I figure he might not recall the old one. Then, flipping through the issue, *Ah I'm not sure I want to look at this stuff.* Surfing stuff, he means. An artefact of life before, washing up in his hands. He wants to chuck it back in to the brain tide. He spends some more time looking at the photos, then goes and gets a surfing book he edited back in the day. He opens one of the big glossy spreads, some dude on some wave, and shows me. Replying like with like,

I guess: *You've got a book of surf photos, me too.*

Out of his book falls a kids' colouring pamphlet featuring animal shapes. He laughs and hands it to me. *Oh yeah, got this one for you – just thought you might enjoy playing with it.* I accept it and readily agree; I mean, I like drawing and I like animals, so. He goes back to *Tracks* and flips to a profile story. *He died a few months ago* he points at the black and white photo of a guy standing beside a board. *Oh?* I say, expecting this to peter out. *He was a shaper, eh?* I ask, testing the information. *Yeah, that's what killed him – the – the*

Fibreglass? I offer.

Yeah.

There is no way for me to verify a few seconds of truth so I take it on face value. Sharp, I think.

The shadow

It becomes clear to me that since the hospitalisation I have become a sort of archetypal Cassidy female to my dad. I can be three or four in quick succession; like a flip book of family photos. Sister, teenage daughter, adult daughter, niece. I imagine his optical recognition of key parts of my face and voice, as a sort of police composite.

I am never *Mum*. I am never his wife.

It's not just face recognition, though. His text messages usually begin with a salutation to me, followed quickly by his younger daughter's name. I play soccer, I surf, I am a woman, a girl, I am the most beautiful, the most wonderful.

Manly

G calls to tell me that Dad's made a panicked phone call, asking for help. He's stranded on Manly beach, where some hooligans have roughed him up and taken his money. He needs directions to home. *Where is home at?*

It's not actually possible, is it? G asks. *I mean, we have to check, don't we?* I call the ward, no answer. I keep checking my voicemail in case the hospital has left a message. Nothing comes, then nothing.

Three weeks ago Dad walked out of the ward to the local train station, boarded a train to Cronulla, presumably ticketless, and walked to his and Mum's recently sold house. Four times.

Now, though, the home inside him has also shifted. The geriatrician asks him where he lives. *With Mum and my sister.* He hasn't lived with his sister since he was a boy. But for a few days I fall into the slippage of the other word. He and I have the most authentic conversation we've ever had, in which he expresses terrible remorse for having left *Mum* behind at home while he ran around doing whatever he liked.

I've not met my half-sister B but since Dad entered the hospital we have talked on the phone a couple of times. It is a cautious but grateful entry into a relationship he had prevented us from having with one another. She tells me of her recent visit to our dad, how as she got up to leave he said, *Can you take me to the station?* She faltered. None of us have inherited his knack for instant fabrication. Before she had a chance to reply, he scratched the thought. *No, you're not going that way, are you.*

38

No one is harmed
The hospital uses an unidentified number, just like the police did a few months ago. Sometimes I feel dread and don't pick up the phone.

They can't punish him
We've had to make an incident report, the nurse says buoyantly, *but no one's been harmed.* They also have to let us know, but there's nothing we can do.

I text C. *Oh my fucking lord! We'll never get him a place if they think he's a sex pest. The family of the other patient could sue him!*

We agree that Mum doesn't need to know about this one. As in life, so in dementia, I say. Eventually C tells Mum anyway. *Lock him away*, she responds dryly.

But I keep seeing the tender little scene, not violent at all, of one body seeking the heat of another. The collapsing of a female presence into something like home, like comfort. And then I pull back from the scene in disgust.

I decide to tell S. *They can't punish him, he's already incarcerated*, she writes.

No one is responding in the way I thought they would.

Fabulous
A new phase of his communication revolves around explaining why he is absent from the outside world.

He is aware, then, that loved ones are elsewhere – and that he is not with them. He is aware that he wants to be or should be with them. But here's the thing: his chronic compulsion to fabricate is alive and well.

The latest messages fall back on familiar tales. *Wish I could be there but the car engine is playing up* or *So sorry I can't get there. The car's been stolen and the police say I shouldn't hold out hope of it being found.*

I tell T how amazed I am that this capacity for deceit is still functioning, since it requires insight. That is, in order to deliberately lie, Dad must be able to understand that another person needs an explanation of his behaviour, and that he doesn't have a reasonable or acceptable explanation for it.

What makes you think he's lying? T responds.

Bloody outrageous

Have you thought about turning off notifications? asks T. She knows I don't answer his messages or calls.

Maybe, I say. *But I like to get a little window into what he's thinking from time to time.*

I reflect on my notion that his confused stories and desperate appeals are somehow informative. What I mean is, are they more or less informative than a magnetic scan to show how shrunken his prefrontal cortex is, or where the big brambles of dead cells lie? Are they more or less informative than a dialogue with him?

This week I am the chosen recipient of his messages for everybody. Once he selects a contact in his text threads then all others are out of sight, as it were.

The latest texts have become increasingly agitated, first asking for times and places to meet; then day by day, hour by hour, more irate exclamations of frustration. He is being imprisoned, held against his will (true); it's outrageous (neither true nor untrue); he just wants to give me a hug (true, even if *I* am someone else).

Despite the synaptic fails, he is bored and lonely. Such feelings aren't only expressed antagonistically; sometimes they come as a torrent of almost euphoric affection. It's this affect that seems to trouble the Broca's area; it's in these moods that he has most trouble finding the words for the feelings. Spelling breaks down in an imaginary flood of oxytocin. His loving message is almost sexual in its panic. The clutter of vocabulary becomes a row of hearts, a rose, a little woman, a rainbow, a little man, a meditating person, kissing lips, a dog, a cat, a clown, a pumpkin, a ghostie.

Behind this door
One Christmas, before his condition was named, he gave me a blank card inside of another blank card.

Hug and kiss you big time
The thread of language that doesn't seem to fray, which keeps strong as a rope, is the catalogue of weasel words he once deployed daily. In cognate life, much of his communication was strung together from phrases in the corporate book of mass communication. Back then, I think it made an innate expressive difficulty much easier for him.

Now it also seems to work when the less exercised, more nuanced sentiments don't transmit. He will help handle the distribution. The team will be there.

There are moves in place. Stuck with a hard load.

There is a company takeover, shitty work problems.

Let's nail the adventure. Go from there.

A solid team talk. Bring on the above. The powers that feed lovely settings with every smart movement, which helps lure people and get them thinking.

A long time between drinks as per
an option to grab
the thick of the situation
works for all
huge hugs
and sunshine desert.

Eclipse

I hear nothing for a week. He's switched to someone else.

Temporarily relieved from that lost voice, I still notice that I'm not chosen.

I wonder if this week's recipient is getting messages addressed to me, just as I get the ones for them. Who is my double?

Before the switch he had begun to transfer the car trouble to me. *We'll be there to help you with the car. No good about your breakdown!*

Maybe he knows something I don't. I go turn the engine over and it's working fine.

ENDER BAŞKAN
THREE POEMS

Ender Başkan is a poet, bookseller and co-founder of Vre Books. He is the author of *A Portrait of Alice as a Young Man*. In 2021, he won the *Overland* Judith Wright Poetry Prize.

funk n wagnalls, collect the set

our neighbours are both mathematicians
they have two girls at school
the younger girl is about 10
walks around churning a rubiks cube
can solve it pretty quick
her dad is proud but says
shes just using a brute force algorithm
soon shell be ready for more a sophisticated one
itll be much faster
damn I think
maybe all i have is brute force
i remember hitting that wall in maths
maybe later than most
but hitting it hard still
and in all these other fields of life too
at least i read a lot as a kid
not so much a canon
but anything with words on it
newspapers
car magazines
womans day
atlases, yellow pages, white pages
books on the deep sea
books on dinosaurs
stats on the back of basketball cards
my parents didnt read books
but they bought them for me
it was the first half of the 90s

i was in primary school
was told by my family that the most important
tools were maths skills
general knowledge
and noticing things
in other words'
problem solving
photo memory
and curiosity
this is a migrants world
wed go over to my grandparents house
and id check my babaannes lotto ticket
wed play cards
my dede would write me up
arithmetic problems
and id ask him questions about the world
like, whats the history of pakistan?
hed have an answer
the world was enormous, i realised
and my world was small
hed stay up every night
reading the turkish encyclopedias
hed brought over when they migrated
my mum was onto it
and started buying me encyclopedias
too from the no frills supermarket at westfield,
airport west
when you spent a certain amount
they were 2 bucks each
we collected the set

and id read them
like my dede did
dipping in anywhere
just to absorb it
but who knows where it went
what this training allowed
my mums mum, my anneanne
got her own set
tho she cant read english
i see them still, thirty years on
high up on her living room shelf
1 11111111111111111111111
every single one is A–American Elk
and American Elk says
–SEE, WAPITI

family holiday

sophie says the way to defeat seasickness
is to look at the horizon
at the urinal im swaying and theres no horizon
only woodgrain wallpaper
i find a speck on it, what is it
how long has it been there and where from
we are on the spirit of tasmania
ezgi is 7 months old
and specks, especially on the floor
mean everything to her
at the cafe one worker says to another
you gotta keep your dignity
never change for anyone
i agree
its not an easy job spiriting tasmania
i wonder if theyre unionised
the boat sways
the boat stinks
on the deck i look down
foam, froth, seeking a speck
i feel the urge to throw a lifebuoy overboard
and watch it disappear
we are on our way to o-bar, eventually
thats how the french onboard say it
dilan and i go to the cafe
for coffee and the worker yells
number 108!
and no one turns up

and they yell it again
and still no one comes
and they yell it again, but even louder
and someone finally comes
this is not what i want my kid to learn
after my long black and her babychino
dilan makes a friend
on the playground
he is a joy
he wants to explore
he wants to pee
he wants to laugh loud
he wants to suck on his toe
his mum is seeing everything as a problem
the only positive reinforcement is when he obeys
then he gets a clap, GOOD JOB!
i learn later shes a casual teacher
sophie and i agree that we are judging her
but not for judgements sake! i say
its for the liberation of children under the yoke
of parents as bosses and managers
not as comrades and guides
over the p.a. it is announced that
poetry will be recited
in the cinema at 230
a soprano will be singing at 300
and a juggler is roaming the ship at all times
it is also announced that the cafe has a pizza oven
margarita hawaiian prosciutto vegetarian
we wander over again

they use a metal spade to slide them in
and play it like a banjo for laughs
we get margarita
cheese so sticky and overwhelming
takes me right back to
tullamarine primary 90–95
pizza 1.50 from the canteen on fridays only
today is friday too, 2023 and the pizza costs 12
not bad i concede
given costa living
i relax
something withers away inside me, like the state
some tasmanian folk give us tips
dont go here, go there
apparently there r roadworks on highway 1
theyre from bagdad, tasmania
the explorer had been reading
arabian nights
i am reading a literary magazine
on the lift down to our car
an older couple looks too intently at ezgi
her lip trembles
she cries

erotics of bookselling

hello were the bookshop where we always say yes
       how can i help you?
              ender speaking
                   how can i help?
                     ender
                         e n d e r
                             ender
                             no no, turkish
                         istanbul ankara baklava
                         so how can i help you?
                             let me look it up
                         bear with me
next please!
                         can i help you?
          would you like a paper bag
                tap on the left
                  have a good day
                     have a nice day
                        have a great day
                come with me and lets see if we
can find it
          we should have it
              let me ask my colleague
              i havent read it but ive heard good things about it
                    youll love this
                      this is great
                          shes great
          i havent read this but ive read her other stuff

i didnt like the last one as much

its been selling like hotcakes

people cant get enough of her

good question

let me look it up on our system

weve got one in stock

i can transfer it

i can get one from the supplier

i can order one in

about two days

about a week

about two weeks

let me calculate it

32.99 39.99 59.99 69.99

nice to meet you

pleased to meet you

good to see you

great to see you

good to hear from you

nice to hear from you

nice shirt

i like your haircut

thanks for that

sorry about that

do you play indoor soccer?

no worries

no stress

no problem at all

nothing to worry about

thats my job

52

                                    thank you
                                        take care
 cheers
        ok, bye now, bye bye
                no, thank you
                    no no, thank you, thanks for coming in
                            im sorry about that
                            thanks for your patience
                theres not much i can do im afraid
                                    im so sorry
                    its out of print
                            it was published in 1803
                        and we last had it in 1997
                if you want to try amazon you know where i stand
 good luck
            i really dont understand the ins and outs of australia post
                its out of my hands really
                                its a big issue, no doubt
                        its systemic
 supply chain
                covid cargo ships
 the exchange rate
 the suez canal the bloody ship didnt run aground it got wedged
        john howards gst
                american express
        we can wrap it for a small donation to our foundation
                            beautiful day out there
                    cold out there
            rainy out there
 wealthy out there

                            53

yeah its a good job
        its fine
            its a market economy
ooo la la
                        nice stack youve got there
i dont mind
        its no big deal
            dont worry
                dont mention it
                    look im sorry
                        my bad
                            its a shame
                            it is what it is
                        its been ages hasnt it?
                            its been a while
                            its been too long
                        its been a pleasure
yeah yeah yeah yeah yeah yeah yeah yeah yeah yeah yeah yeah
        yes yes yes
            yes we can
                        the customer is always the customer
        ok bye, bye, bye, bye, thank you, baa-bye, bye, bye
love you, ok, bye, thank you, thank you, yeah i will, yeah say hi
too, bye, bye now, see you later, bye, love you, mwah
                        can you say hi to everyone for me?
            say hello
        send my regards
send my love
        say hi
            hit me up

text me

call me   anything

drop in

ill swing by

see you soon

love u

take care

ciao

bye

ANTIGONE KEFALA
LAST JOURNALS

Wednesday, 5 January 2022

A new year.

Let's hope for more positive news – not evident in the number of people infected.

Humid and warm. Overcast.

The city has remained empty for such a long time now...only the cars on the bridge moving.

We started the year with hospitals – scans yesterday at Carillion Avenue – emptiness there too...

They gave us the large envelope with the prints of the back scan, will see what the doctor says on Thursday...

Hoping for less pain and some energy to deal with other issues.

Will put together last year's notebook today and try and read it. Is there something alive and of importance – I doubt it – only complaints probably.

Will see...

Next Monday, or maybe the weekend if I feel better, start to read the pages of *Late Journals* – hopefully not too many errors.

Barbara wants to be here when the doctor comes tomorrow, to see what the scan is showing and what direction...

Will have to look at the Christmas cards and respond.

Some progress – I am at least capable of coming here, staying in the chair and typing.

Alexander came to check on me...am I ok...

He is trying to speak to David to clean his garden a bit.

Friday, 7 January 2022
Made it to the studio.
A nice breeze blowing in the garden.

Still tired. I have read the manuscript once, but have to read it again. Not enough concentration.

A gun seems to go off, reminds me of Adelaide, the festival, and we in the country, near the lake with the ducks.

I can't put myself together and begin to do some work.

Victoria, Marike and Isabella have covid.

Decided today to stop taking all medication and see the result. I AM NOT TAKING THAT MANY. The one in the morning and then some stronger panadols...
The fundamental issue is that I am not feeling well – the back, the scan shows my spine in a bad way...what improvement is possible?

Must go up. Tired already...hope to come tomorrow.

My head buzzing with the news of the world, all bad, covid, possible war – Russia and Ukraine, everyone up in arms.

Thinking all the time of friends that have gone, James, Jolanta and Jurgis – travelling in the country, Australia Day at La Perouse...

Gail sent a card made by her husband – I should start doing some drawings...

When am I going to start doing some work?

Sent the blue book to Patricia in Melbourne...she will like it...was alarmed that I did not get in touch for some time, rang...

Thursday, 20 January 2022
Suddenly a day full of black thoughts, old, not well and no future.

Eating rice for the whole day, trying to find a direction, feeling alone in this wet, sticky atmosphere.
    No energy to see how I shall cope with everything.

Reading again and again the manuscript – nothing there somehow.

I seem to have something wrong with me physically that can't be fixed. Well yesterday, sick today.
    I have not felt that low for a long time.
    Already the month has almost gone and what have I done with it?

Thank God for Eleni and Bob. They come full of energy and good will, bringing food, soups, doing the shopping...

I have not written anything for ages, no energy at all... Doctors, scans, my back in a bad way, vitamin D that is supposed to be good for my bones not accepted by my stomach.

Since I pushed myself to finish *Late Journals* I have not been well.

I was not aware how intellectual pressures transform into physical difficulties.

At night unable to sleep making plans, all illusions of what I do, but really I am no longer capable of doing much. Was sending an email to Penelope to ask what progress...

Thought of James, Miuta, look them up online – Miu will not be there...

Too distressing to write about them, this is why Jurgis went back to drawing, he found writing too dangerous...

Must make a program, begin to do something, already a month of the new year has gone...and what have I done? Complaints.

Very preoccupied with the body...my terrible back, the pain, the fact that I can't walk that much.

Displeased with myself, my constant dependence now on other people, the ongoing direction...

Having to accept more and more a diminishing capability to do things and so on...

Thursday, 27 January 2022
Yesterday a lovely day, Eleni and Bob dropped by on their way to lunch, we did a bit of shopping, stayed on the terrace with the nice breeze, a lonely jet in the sky making a tremendous noise... The TV full of patriotic feelings...

At night I watched a long program by Michael Portillo on Australia – read as I went upstairs, but then I could not sleep for three quarters of the night...one, two, three, four, struggling with everything...finally fell asleep around five, had to get up early as Robert was coming to clean at eight-thirty.

Very tired waiting for them to finish so that I can go to bed.

Barbara is supposed to come in the afternoon by bus...going to the dentist...

Doing nothing. I read the manuscript three times, every time I found another error. I am giving it up now, will send an email to Ivor to ask him how I should send it back – post it etc., etc.

Mild morning, humid, feeling slightly better. I hope it lasts... Beth came yesterday, brought fried fish...will take me to the hairdresser, Kelly will cut the hair. Darren not well, a stomach operation, I hope he is better...

Mary rang from Athens to see how I was... It was snowing for two days, images of an *evzone* below the parliament with snow over his face. Mary did not seem to be impressed with the snow. All the kids are well, Pandeli travelling, they have a little girl.

Must make a program, tidy the will and so on.

Wednesday, 2 February 2022
Still very humid but cooler.

Trying to get rid of papers, Jim was still sending me photos, texts and so on, but now, not very much... We are all slowing down.

Evelyn and Ivor came on Sunday – they took away the manuscript of *Late Journals*. Discussions about other things, he is thinking about publishing a collection of all my poems... A COLLECTED...

Left some of his recent books – poetry mostly – I have not read them yet, prose Jessica Au – *Cold Enough for Snow*...a small scale, detailed observations, a very cool tone...

I wonder if this is the new tone of prose...must read all the books to have some idea of the new direction...

Always lovely to see them. We fall into talking in a friendly way, Ivor is struggling with all his new publishing plans including the magazine...

Evelyn is writing about an ornithologist Chisholm? Some such name.

Waiting for Barbara to read *The Dancer* so that I can continue with it, but sad, the heroine died young...

Trying to arrange things – my medical direction, tackle the will again...

Define yet again this propensity to write journals – an ongoing conversation with oneself, the inner necessity to define to a certain extent one's relationship with the events of one's life...

EVERYTHING REMINDS ONE OF THE PAST...

Thursday, 3 February 2022

A more difficult period is starting now, more dependence on others to do things, everyone's ideas of how or what should be done and so on.

Annie ringing this morning was complaining of the same thing. But what can be done seeing that we don't have enough energy to deal with things ourselves.

Feeling slightly better for the moment...it may not last...

Post knitting to Lalo, clean papers.

Look at poems to see what is there, have something ready if Ivor decides to do a collected.

Tired already with all the people I have to deal with, their personalities...an opening for them in which they can do something, and then a closing when they have other obligations, one has to adjust to these changes continuously.

Tired now...

Monday, 7 February 2022
To town with Eleni and Bob, walked for quite a while looking for a comfortable chair.

Depressing sights – the same design and colour, off-white, everywhere, grey...an uninteresting colour.

Found a more modest chair, vibrant dark blue, bought it $800 plus $100 for delivery.

I hope it goes well with the rest of the colours in the front room.

Take this one upstairs and get rid of the red one, which has become very old.

Very tired, they too, humid and raining.

A bellicose atmosphere in the world, the TV full of negative news, terrible happenings, the elderly not given much care, current ministers totally uninterested in their duties.

Dutton on TV blah blahing away, for a long time, a terrible face, eyes and head...

I, tired with everyone, everyone giving me advice what to eat, what medication to take, what to do with my life.

Annie was complaining about this too, obviously the new direction and more of it to come.

I must become more silent, keep things to myself, they too, poor things have to respond to my complaints.

Some silence.

Sunday, 13 February 2022

Sleep a lot with the new pills.

Make everyday programs of what I am going to do – but not doing anything.

Marie's book has arrived looking good – gave copies to Eleni and Bob.

Must send some money to George – waiting to speak to Helen, match what she sent.

Not enough energy to do much.

The new chair in the front room has arrived, very comfortable and a lovely deep blue colour.

Tuesday, 15 February 2022

Everyone is desperate.

Martha yesterday, talking to me as if I could help her, but her troubles with Peter more desperate than any of us. And I full of problems – my back, my stomach, now my eyes...

Must ring Anna for the name and telephone number of our

eye doctor, I hope she and Hilik are ok.

Ring Ileana…

Must eat more, I have lost three pounds.

Marie's book has arrived and looks good.

George's afterword moving. He came to bring the books.

We stayed on the terrace and had coffee. Things are okay with Blaise.

Human presences continue to be encouraging.

Friday, 18 February 2022

Very hot and humid.

Everyone anxious. Anna Y unable to sleep…her dogs…

Dogs are becoming a major nuisance.

A documentary on the Japanese, young women treating them as their children, dressing them up, etc. etc.…

Vrasidas is launching his book on Angelopoulos, invited to the launch, send an email, order the book from Gleebooks.

Not an idea in my head.

The photocopier run out of ink, will go with Lenore and buy some.

Looking at the advice of Kant on my wall: have something to do, someone to love and something to hope for…

Except for the first the other two rather difficult to achieve.

Thursday, 24 February 2022

Waiting for Robert to come and clean, he is nearly half an hour late.

Who knows what happened everywhere with the rain, masses of it, the wind.

WET... WET...

Dark as well.

Will go with Lenore to do some shopping...not very enthusiastic about it.

Disasters and wars everywhere – Ukraine...the Russians...Putin and so on.

Waiting for Robert to arrive, already nine o'clock...

Small birds in the garden shaking their wings in the rain.

Robert sent a message about traffic...ten past nine... Dark and wet...

Began reading old and new copies of *Limelight* – I have not been reading them for some time. Music and musicians going on...

Robert and his assistant have just arrived. Lenore is coming at eleven, or after.

Lots of letters to answer but not moving on anything...to Wendy, Robyn, Diana, Vezili, and so on...

What I would like to do now is go to bed and have a little sleep.

Sunday, 27 February 2022

Fighting the whole afternoon with the photocopier – installed the new inks, tried again and again to follow instructions but still I don't make it, the machine refuses to start. I was hoping to do it myself and not ask Bob to look at it tomorrow...

What it tells me is that there is a foreign object in the machine. But there is no foreign object inside it, unless I have not noticed some minor detail...

Tired of it.

At least the rain has stopped today, but still very muggy and wet.

Constantly having to do things – answer email; write letters, last night the light in the kitchen went out, rang Harry, he came today and fixed it...on and on...

Medication – what I have to take, put everything down so that I know what is happening.

To the chemist tomorrow to pick up the new lot...write everything down.

Machines!!!!!

I seem to be full of plans of what I am supposed to do but do very little.

Everyone is sending emails – Penelope – photos of the wedding, Anna Y photos of the two dogs in their elegant box, Dennis a long poem about Newtown and Vegemite, and so on...

In the meantime Russia has invaded Ukraine, refugees, but Putin goes on with his dreams of grandeur...

Tuesday, 1 March 2022
First of March, Mărțișor.

Rain and more rain, flooding everywhere. Large objects travelling in the flooded rivers, people walking in high waters in groups, they look as if they are coming from an Angelopoulos film...

I always think of Mihail Sadoveanu, and *Venea o moară pe Siret*... should google it...

Barbara was coming but with this weather...spoke to her, she was looking at all the arrangements with social services, she wants to activate everything so that I can ask for a few hours of help. We will see.

Report about the state of the world – not good at all...we have destroyed everything – but who is listening??

Should write some letters.

Try and walk to the postal box to see if I can do it, I have lost my courage...that's it, in a nutshell – as they will say.

Eleni still working on Lawrence's portrait – she is working on the buttons of his shirt – a slow progression.

Wednesday, 2 March 2022

Rain and more rain. Flooding, the rivers rising, streets full of destroyed stuff waiting to be collected.

Suddenly, while typing now, the sun came out for a few seconds. I have not solved the problem with the photocopy machine. MACHINES...terrible things...

And I not doing anything.

Dried clothes on the heater the whole morning – smell of stale water everywhere. Beth and Warwick left for their holiday a few days ago, stopped by waters, coming back today...

Dark political news – Putin advancing into Ukraine... Sanctions on him, but he does not care...

Once the army comes in and weapons – things are lost...

Thursday, 3 March 2022

The sun came out, momentarily, everything brighter, then the clouds came over and rain came down, sifting through the air.

Looking over the city, a white curtain.

Rang Franco. He was waiting for me to ring, apparently I had promised, I can't remember it, preoccupied with the rain, the light in the kitchen not quite working, afraid that water has come through the electricity line and so on...

Franco coming for coffee next Thursday, must put together all the papers I kept for him.

All the mail, now that Bob has transferred all accounts online, just to tell me that they have taken money from my account.

Must look at:

All payments, mark them on my cheque book!

Look at all account papers.

Clean the drawer.

Sad about everything – the rain, the destruction here, houses, furniture and so on, Franco's Elizabeth who can't find words, anymore – so that she can speak...

A slow disintegration of all of us.

Sad that Barbara always insists that I must shop online, not allow Bob to do the shopping. I am too dependent on Eleni and Bob they will get tired of the burden. She is probably right, but so far, they seem to be okay with it. I like human involvement, all this online business...

Friday, 4 March 2022

Mushrooms growing on the lawn.

Sparkling white and very fresh.

I assume the whole of New South Wales is covered in mushrooms...

The rain had stopped for an hour, but now is ready to start again.

I have been looking at letters I have to answer for a week now, but not doing anything about it.

Waiting for the rain to stop, for the sun to come out, to start doing something.

This morning, a very battered envelope I sent to Nikos with the book of essays, was returned. I must check again the address, write to Diana to thank her for the Stylianos book, to Robyn, to Wendy...maybe I should ring her, see if I have a telephone number.

Saturday, 5 March 2022

Still raining.

Helen rang, sad, her younger son, his wife and the two kids have decided to move to Ballina for a year, a change of scene...with the rain and so on, they are looking for sun and hot weather – but Ballina now, under water...

Helen very fond of the little boy, was looking after him for some time as both parents were working.

I would like to send her something to cheer her up, but what? Told her that Ivor is sending the manuscript to the printers, will send her a copy.

Helen sounded discouraged – but I am old – she is only in her seventies.

Barbara working to put me on the social services list for possible help but it seems, at the beginning, what they give you is two hours a fortnight, so much effort for so little.

Sunday, 6 March 2022
The only thing that I can do – with alacrity – is sleep. Especially during the day.

Had lunch, slept.

Must make a cup of tea.

The thin roses – small, on the terrace, look like invalids.

Barbara working to give me medicine and new mechanical additions to walk better... WALKERS – looked them up on Google, quite stunned at the idea that I could use them.

Thursday, 10 March 2022
Finally the rain has stopped today. How long will it last. Nothing but smell of stale water and mould.

New South Wales full of water, destroyed household things,

people in distress and Scomo spending money to enlarge the army.

Apparently this is going to be his topic in the election – safety...

Obviously, with so much destruction everywhere. But people destroyed by floods are unhappy at the lack of help...

I should start doing some drawings, at least my attention will be taken away from all these killings on TV.

Monday, 14 March 2022
Opened the window
the sounds of the city
birds flying in the morning light.

Autumn, silence
as if nature too is resting
not one single cloud in the sky
after so much rain.

Thursday, 17 March 2022
Woke up tired,
Came down, had breakfast, decided to lie down and rest.

Rang Anne B.
Distressed. She fell yesterday, was on the floor for two hours waiting for Bianca to come, then they waited for an ambulance. How careful we all must be not to fall – we all know that. Trying to encourage each other...

Tuesday, 29 March 2022
Budget night.

The washing machine has arrived and Eleni put it on. Next Monday – see if I can learn how to use it.

It dried the washing – they looked okay.

Today, a lot of things – in the morning, a nurse, I assume, came to take blood. I had to get up early, waited for her at seven o'clock, people trying to be sociable, pleasant.

Ordered towels from Innovations.

The war in Ukraine going on, bombings, cities destroyed – the Russians must be mad – Putin: Why suddenly this desire to conquer more, to grow bigger??

In the meantime – the BBC program last night on Four Corners, how we have destroyed nature, and how we go on destroying it. All the signs are there, terrible floods, winds, and so on, but in spite of all this we are still not doing anything about it... What about future generations?

Reading the *TLS*...the British Empire...the tone has become more cautious, not as full of hype as before.

SBS must be out of money...many programs on the British Crown.

I imagine they buy them at discounts... Even on the ABC, little about the arts.

Sunday, 3 April 2022

Politics all around. Elections coming. Everyone knocking out Morrison...his own people, a pity they did not do it before.

The sun out for the moment. The clocks had to be readjusted.
  Tired.
  Everything looks mouldy and neglected.
  It will take some time to dry out, but the rain will start again in a little while.

Monday, 11 April 2022

BOOK OUT!

Looking at will... Literary executors, etc.... Arranging for things after you die, an equally difficult problem.
  Very tired after the weekend – the excitement of the book appearing, Ivor and Evelyn in the house bringing books, the presence of the book, contracts that have to be signed...

Living is problematic, but dying is problematic too.

Wednesday, 13 April, 2022

Looking for a book to start translating something – this should give me a direction... Looked at Rilke and Malte... Rather sad, the whole thing.
  People ringing. Efi, yesterday, using the mobile so that we could see our faces. These terrible transformations...who wants to see one's face when talking on the phone...
  I was hoping that someone will say something about the new book – but so far no one has picked it up, as if it does not exist...

The whole public field as it appears in the *Herald* and on TV a heavy, uninteresting, ordinary approach to things.

This British pragmatism that here does not have any other form except self-interest and that too of a very mediocre kind.

Faute de mieux – voting for Albanese...

Saturday, 16 April 2022
EASTER – emptiness and silence...

Sunday, 17 April 2022
Heavy fog in the morning, now opening up, a sort of NZ atmosphere.

No one about. At David's a lot of movement yesterday. He is moving out, going to his daughter and son-in-law, and the young ones are coming here.

The terrace full of stuff he is taking with him – bed etc.

But what is happening with Nick, the cat.

What year was I born, thirty-one I said. You are ninety!!! she said. Who wants to discuss my age. Tired of it.

Watching political discussions on the ABC. Boring personalities, populist political decisions, nothing to engage one's mind or ideas.

Not one real idea or view of the future.

The political scene here quite brutal.

Morrison the image of the field and whatever subtlety, complexity it still had totally crushed by his populism, his smug attitude to issues, and a total field of mediocrities.

Must stop watching so much TV – political issues which are not fundamentally speaking of any real political impact, but just mediocre minds pretending to have some attitudes.

Thursday, 21 April 2022
The Greek Colonels Day, I think.

I trying to recover from the eye intervention, I assume, I should call it, operation too extreme a word.

Early in the studio, Robert and his assistant in the house cleaning.

The sun out and white cockatoos rushing about.

The sun *clipocind* on the wall.

Greek Easter coming up. Vrasidas wanted us to do something. I sent him an email to tell him that I have not been well. To come for coffee.

Sunday, 24 April 2022
Eleni and Bob here bringing tsoureki, red eggs.

David has left the house.

Lights in the house show empty walls, empty rooms, painters in the house, his granddaughters are coming to live here, they are studying at Sydney Uni.

Coming back to my eyes – the doctor said that they are healthy, a laser treatment on the right, everything seems ok.

Paul has been in touch, email, suggesting we meet and go to the gallery, have lunch there – but who has the energy??

Asked him to come for coffee, he sent me photos of the family

– their Easter gathering, painted eggs, two new little children that I don't recognise...

Saturday, 7 May 2022
Yesterday – the first carer came, a nice person of Lebanese heritage – as one would say.

Posted all the books that I thought I should send: Patricia, Martha, Vassy, Dennis and Lola.

Heavy to carry and slightly problematic at the post office with my lack of energy. But done.

Will see what others I shall send.

Decide on a program:

Translations?

Old writings that must be destroyed or worked on.

Look at 2021 diary – see if there is anything there – a page that I can send to Ivor for his magazine.

Sunday, 15 May 2022
The sun is out.

Wet everywhere.

Ordered some clothes from Innovations.

Email to Lenore.

Must send email to Martha to thank her for the flowers.

Spoke to Eleni – all okay there.

Trying to clean papers – but difficult to breathe in the studio.

Friday, 20 May 2022
Very, very tired, hardly able to stand.

A day full of troubles – not really, but not that good.

RAIN, RAIN, rain and cold.

Electricity off for two hours in the morning.

The carer came with another person, a student that will become a carer.

Going from place to place with two people after you – bank, post office. Then shopping, coming home in the rain, totally pleased to be alone.

A sandwich for lunch, then to bed. Electricity people here, more rain.

Bought magazines, papers, etc.

The atmosphere charged with the coming election. I have voted by post.

Scomo everywhere, I hope we can get rid of him, he has lowered the tone of the place to zero, not an idea in the air only waffle produced with a totally convincing tone.

Will see what happens tomorrow.

I am afraid to believe that we will finally get rid of him. Nothing but political mediocrities around him.

Rest. So tired, must take it easy.

Remember election nights at Elizabeth's with all the friends, sitting together in her apartment, some nights of success and some of disappointment.

Elizabeth – fiercely to Labor.

All gone now – Jolanta, Jurgis and so on.

Images tonight on TV of Singleton where they photographed me...Broken Hill and so on...

Sunday, 22 May 2022

A program on the ABC about Cobar and a musical happening in a water tank, very good, very Australian…

Look to see if I have written anything about Cobar, any photos? If it were not for my adventurous friends, I would not have seen the outback in any real sense.

Ivor sent email – a small review of the book in *The Saturday Paper*.

On the ABC religious singing.

The rain has stopped for a moment but it will start again.

We are all exhausted after all the political happenings, Scomo finally gone, a lot of Liberals lost their seats and ALBO is in.

Will see what the future will bring.

The review in *The Saturday Paper* quite positive.

Everyone feels positive – that is friends – about the possibilities of the future.

On TV – the program from London: 'People that have lived here – Peckham – in less than favourable circumstances.'

The ultimate polite description of a terrible poverty.

SBS: American music – Joplin – 'That is not a record, is an experience.'

Wednesday, 8 June 2022

Last Monday Homer's birthday.

Cold, windy and very dry. The house in a mess.

The builder came today and injected some fluid into the brick to help it dry.

Eleni and Bob here for a few days in the morning, speaking to the builder.

We bought a small vacuum cleaner for the studio.

Have done nothing...totally preoccupied with walls, cleaning and so on.

I can't imagine when the house will be cleaned and arranged to enjoy it.

Albanese – doing his duties – Indonesia etc.

At least we don't have to worry about Scomo – but things are not very good, inflation, higher interest rates... All the mess left by Scomo now has to be cleaned up by Albanese.

Thursday, 9 June 2022
In the studio getting rid of old papers – shredding them.

From time to time reading all these entries...getting rid of papers as if I am getting rid of my life.

Too much accumulation...

Very cold. The house in a mess,

Scrapped walls, furniture moved. Cold and unfriendly. This morning a smell of gas.

Rang Eleni, she checked with the company...all in order – this is what happens when they disconnect it for work.

Will go up now. Have a coffee to reassure ourselves that life goes on.

Cold wind, empty streets, strong sunlight... Winter.

Monday, 11 July 2022

Not very good news today. Barbara has been diagnosed with breast cancer – at the beginning of the process, let's hope that they can cure it expeditiously, as they say...

Every day more dark news – rain, and more rain, people trying to put their lives together...and now Barbara.

The medical assessors are coming on Wednesday to discuss my problems...

People writing, asking questions about the past the Australia Council and so on.

Harvey is trying to put his past in order, asking questions... when I was there, when I worked with Jean, is she still alive and so on...

Last night dreamt of Jurgis, for the first time we were looking at each other, he seemed in a good mood...

Thursday, 14 July 2022

Yesterday a full day. They came for the ASSESSMENT. A nice, polite woman, questions again, all taken down...the responses... what am I capable of doing...walking etc., etc....

Thank God Eleni and Bob are here so that I don't feel that exposed.

My skin in a bad way, all flared up and very itchy – putting cream on it all the time but little effect.

Bad news in every direction...

Last night the ABC broadcast a concert from the Opera House, they finished repairs. The place looking very good.

The Resurrection symphony...this is what I need... resurrection...

The world full of disasters – famine, fires, rain and so on... The TV is feeding us with all the negative information...and I, somehow, cannot bring myself to look at more positive DVDs.

Must take it slowly. Try not to be so nervous.

The streets empty and silent. Above a pale blue sky...

Friday, 22 July 2022

The rain has stopped for a little while – late afternoon, the sky has cleared to a pale blue.

Eleni and Bob here helping me to clear things, Alexander came to fix the little bar in the kitchen to hang the small towels...

It will be nice when September comes and we can paint the place and clean it up– later outside too.

Running around, lose things – my glasses, I had to bring my second pair from upstairs – where do I put them? A mystery.

Getting rid of papers but still a lot to go on. Lack of energy. Better in the afternoon than in the morning.

Long disturbed nights, in and out of bed constantly.

I have not slept for a whole night for a long time, afraid to take something, my whole nervous apparatus quite frail.

The studio wet, all the paint full of blisters, especially on the right side.

Saturday, 30 July 2022
Looking at the articles in *Kosmos* – the last few ones about Yota and me. I should photocopy one or two pages and send them to Helen, she is being left out...

   Michelakakis used one of James' photos.

I have not been feeling well. Cystitis – I have to drink this terrible pink liquid.

Silence in the neighbourhood, the young women next door are having a party tonight, they left a note, the music will stop at 11 p.m....

Constantly undecided, going over and over everything... The will – looking at it as if I have not seen it before and have to constantly adjust it. Have I included everyone? Have I left things to all? Have I forgotten anyone? And so on...

Constantly not enough energy to deal with things properly... postponing...postponing...

Empty afternoon.

Wednesday, 3 August 2022
AUGUST – the month that was always good for writing.
   Little happening now.

Outside warmer than inside – a sunny afternoon, everything very dry.

Watered the garden.

The studio full of wet walls.

Doing nothing... Full of plans that I never carry out.

Yesterday with Eleni and Bob to town, in the park in Watsons Bay, talking of the past – Usher, our first flat together in Rose Bay...

The past, talking about it, a tiring affair...

Cystitis still on.

Losing weight – sixty kilos now from seventy...sixty-eight...and so on...

The world goes on...tragedies, wars...

Lots of typing errors the white cover-up not working...

Let it be now.

Tuesday, 9 August 2022

We celebrated Eleni's birthday today – I gave her one of Leonida's sculptures, the black bronze one.

Going to a good home.

Must give the glass little sculpture to Anna – she liked it. A lot of movement today. Indra was here too, she is going to Nepal for three months in September.

After they left I went to bed. Getting tired more often now.
 Silence and empty streets.

Not looking at papers, not putting anything in order either.

Thursday, 4 August 2022
Robert and his assistant in the house cleaning.
 I waiting to have a coffee and lie down.
 My constant direction now.

I must speak to Dr A, but every time I ring she is not there, away…
they put me through to C, but I don't want to speak to him. He
has not been helpful in the past.

August already – maybe the spring will make us feel better.

On the ABC last night, a program on TREES – living for eight
hundred, one thousand years and so on. I forgot to ask Eleni if
she saw it. She is working on TREES…

From the studio – the garden very neat and peaceful. I must go
and have some lunch.
 Sunshine and empty streets.

Tuesday, 23 August 2022
Sunny, very cold day.

Waiting for the rain that they say is coming for a week from
now.
 Not doing anything, complaining to myself!

Washed clothes put them out to dry for some sun and wind on them.

Constantly using the machine now.

Lebanon in the news again, some destroyed parts of the port, etc., etc.

The local news full of Scomo and his nefarious directions. Appointing himself to six portfolios and so on. Minister of this, of that and so on. Surreal, the whole thing.

How quickly, even in a system that seems to be okay, you have changes that one did not think possible –

Thursday, 1 September 2022
Spring already.

A nice breeze blowing.

Enmeshed in all my difficulties.

Dithering all the time. Cancelled my meeting with Lenore, not enough energy for it.

Reza in the house, Eleni arranging what has to be done.

Skirting boards out and now to be put back.

Taking pills, forgetting to take them, seeing no improvement.

The ginger cat from next door, a new arrival, in the garden taking note of all the sounds.

Must go up now and do some cooking.

Saturday, 10 September 2022

Very tired, wobbly –

All these happenings that seem to take my strength away.

DEATHS – the Queen, all these funeral rituals that they show us on TV on and on. People waiting for twenty hours to see the Queen in her coffin and so on...

Ivor ringing yesterday to tell me that I won the Patrick White Literary Award – the same that Elizabeth won.

Before we would have been very glad...but now...everyone gone.

Told Eleni – she was very pleased.

Will wait for a week to tell a few others.

Annoyed at the idea that I will have to face some people that will come to discuss the issue.

Everything comes in its own time – but not in yours.

Great emptiness in the street and a thin sun.

Television – an empty medium.

Monday, 19 September 2022

The garden looks very neat – Alexander worked on it this morning.

Sunny and windy.

Trying to put myself together.

The Queen's funeral has finished, thank God.

The only thing I seem to want to do is lie down and go to sleep, have coffees or eat chocolate.

I should take something to give myself a boost – Barbara was suggesting some heroin but in my case it will probably kill me.

The cave full of wet walls, everything looking like me – devastated. Ivor wonders if he should publish a few more copies of the poems, in view of the prize.

Drifting... Not an ounce of focused energy...

New Titles from Giramondo

Fiction

Sanya Rushdi *Hospital*
Alexis Wright *Praiseworthy*
Shaun Prescott *The Town*
Jon Fosse *Septology* (trans. Damion Searls)
Shaun Prescott *Bon and Lesley*
George Alexander *Mortal Divide*: *The Autobiography of Yiorgos Alexandroglou*
Luke Carman *An Ordinary Ecstasy*
Norman Erikson Pasaribu *Happy Stories, Mostly* (trans. Tiffany Tsao)
Jessica Au *Cold Enough for Snow*
Max Easton *The Magpie Wing*

Non-fiction

Imants Tillers *Credo*
Bastian Fox Phelan *How to Be Between*
Antigone Kefala *Late Journals*
Evelyn Juers *The Dancer: A Biography for Philippa Cullen*
Gerald Murnane *Last Letter to a Reader*
Anwen Crawford *No Document*

Poetry

Grace Yee *Chinese Fish*
Autumn Royal *The Drama Student*
Lucy Dougan *Monster Field*
Michael Farrell *Googlecholia*
Lisa Gorton *Mirabilia*
Zheng Xiaoqiong *In the Roar of the Machine* (trans. Eleanor Goodman)
Lionel Fogarty *Harvest Lingo*
Tracy Ryan *Rose Interior*
Claire Potter *Acanthus*
Adam Aitken *Revenants*
J.S. Harry *New and Selected Poems*
Andy Jackson *Human Looking*

For more information visit giramondopublishing.com.

Acknowledgements

We respectfully acknowledge the Gadigal, Burramattagal and Cammeraygal peoples, the traditional owners of the lands where Giramondo's offices are located. We extend our respects to their ancestors and to all First Nations peoples and Elders.

HEAT Series 3 Number 9 has been prepared in collaboration with Ligare Book Printers and Candida Stationery; we thank them for their support.

The Giramondo Publishing Company is grateful for the support of Western Sydney University in the implementation of its book publishing program.

Giramondo Publishing is assisted by the Australian Government through the Australia Council for the Arts.

This project is supported by the Copyright Agency's Cultural Fund.

HEAT Series 3
Editor Alexandra Christie
Designer Jenny Grigg
Typesetter Andrew Davies
Copyeditor Aleesha Paz
Marketing Manager Kate Prendergast
Publishers Ivor Indyk and Evelyn Juers
Associate Publisher Nick Tapper

Editorial Advisory Board
Chris Andrews, Mieke Chew, J.M. Coetzee, Lucy Dougan, Lisa Gorton,
Bella Li, Tamara Sampey-Jawad, Suneeta Peres da Costa, Alexis Wright
and Ashleigh Young.

Contact
For editorial enquiries, please email
heat.editor@giramondopublishing.com.
Follow us on Instagram @HEAT.lit and
Twitter @HEAT_journal.

Accessibility
We understand that some formats will not be accessible to all readers.
If you are a reader with specific access requirements, please contact
orders@giramondopublishing.com.

For more information, visit giramondopublishing.com/heat.

Published June 2023
from the Writing and Society Research Centre
at Western Sydney University
by the Giramondo Publishing Company
Locked Bag 1797
Penrith NSW 2751 Australia
www.giramondopublishing.com

This collection © Giramondo Publishing 2023
Typeset in Tiempos and Founders Grotesk Condensed
designed by Kris Sowersby at Klim Type Foundry

Printed and bound by Ligare Book Printers
Distributed in Australia by NewSouth Books

A catalogue record for this book is available from
the National Library of Australia.

HEAT Series 3 Number 9
ISBN: 978-1-922725-08-0
ISSN: 1326-1460

ISBN 978-1-922725-08-0

9 781922 725080 >